D0150367

HOUGHTON MIFFLIN

Reading

A Legacy of Literacy

Incredible STORIES

HOUGHTON MIFFLIN   BOSTON · MORRIS PLAINS, NJ

California · Colorado · Georgia · Illinois · New Jersey · Texas

Design, Art Management and Page Production: Kirchoff/Wohlberg, Inc.

ILLUSTRATION CREDITS
4-21 David Murphy. **22-39** Krystyna Stasiak. **40-57** Mary GrandPré.
58-75 Suling Wang.

Copyright © 2001 by Houghton Mifflin Company. All rights reserved.

No part of this work may be reproduced or transmitted in any form or by
any means, electronic or mechanical, including photocopying and recording,
or by any information storage or retrieval system without the prior written
permission of Houghton Mifflin Company unless such copying is expressly
permitted by federal copyright law. Address inquiries to School Permissions,
Houghton Mifflin Company, 222 Berkeley Street, Boston, MA 02116.

Printed in U.S.A.

ISBN: 0-618-04391-8

789-VH-05 04 03 02

Incredible STORIES

Contents

Robocat

by
Andrew Clements

illustrated by
Dave Murphy

Strategy Focus

As you read the story, stop once in a while to **evaluate** how the author shows that Robocat is a fantasy cat.

It was a beautiful summer day.
But something didn't feel right.
Robocat could smell crime
in the air.

Robocat looked between the rows
of vegetables. He looked all
around the garden.

Then he said, "Someone's been tasting the turnips. Someone's been crunching the carrots. This looks like a job for Robocat!"

That night Robocat hid in a tree by the garden. He said, "These crooks don't have a chance."

Z Z Z Z Z Z

Robocat watched the garden all night long.
Well, almost all night long.

The next morning Robocat went down
to the garden. More turnips and carrots
were gone!

Robocat saw holes, lots of holes, under the fence. He said, "Someone's been digging under the fence! Someone's been playing dirty!"

Robocat filled all the holes. Then he stood very still in the garden. He waited for something to happen.

"These crooks think they're pretty smart," he said. "But not when Robocat is on the case!"

That night, Robocat heard digging and
nibbling. Someone saw Robocat. Someone
laughed and said, "Would you look at that!
I'm sooooo scared!"

Suddenly Robocat flipped on his lights.
He said, "You should be scared. I'm Robocat!
Stay right where you are!"

15

It was Patch Rabbit and the Hoppers!
Robocat said, "Paws up! I have you at last!"

Patch Rabbit said, "Not so fast, Tuna Breath. Do you have us or do we have you?"

"And now we know the answer!" said Robocat. "Like I said, I have you. And now you are all going to spend some time with the chickens."

Patch Rabbit said, "We will find a way out of here, I promise! And when we do, we will eat every vegetable in the garden!"

Robocat said, "Not while Robocat's watching!"

Patch smiled. "We can wait until you take a catnap," he said.

Thinking About the Selection

1. What are Patch Rabbit and the Hoppers doing in the garden?

2. Tell about one part of the story that could really happen and one part that couldn't.

Is It Real or Is It Fantasy ?

There are some things a real cat can do and some things only a fantasy cat can do. Think of some of each of those things. Then write them on a chart like this.

Real cats can	Fantasy cats can
meow	talk

21

The Dragon of Krakow

A Polish folktale

adapted by Maryann Dobeck
illustrated by Krystyna Stasiak

Strategy Focus

A hungry dragon comes to town. As you read, think of **questions** to discuss.

Long ago there was a little village in Poland that had no name. The people who lived there worked so hard, they had no time to think of one!

Every morning a rooster crowed at the rising sun. When the villagers heard his "kru, kru, kru," they woke up.

They had to get up very early because there
was so much work to do.

The farmer fed the pigs.
The milkmaid milked the cows.
The butcher made sausages.

The baker made cakes, rolls, and pies.
The woodsman cut down trees.

But one morning the rooster woke up late.
Smoke covered everything. It blocked
out the sun. Day was as black as night.

When the rooster saw the dark day and smelled the smoke, he began to crow. He crowed "kru, kru, kru" ten times louder than ever before. The villagers came out to see what was the matter.

The villagers could see bright flames down by the river.

"The forest must be on fire!" yelled the woodsman.

A young man named Krakus called out,
"Follow me, and we will see!"

Krakus and the villagers went down
to the river.

On the edge of the river was a dragon.
He was covered with scales.
He had rows of long, pointy teeth.
Flames and smoke came out of his mouth.

"I'm hungry!" roared the dragon. "Bring me the best foods in the land. Then make me your king, or I will eat you up!"

"What can we do?" cried the villagers.

"I have a plan," said Krakus. "Just do as I say. I'll need help from all of you."

Krakus asked the villagers for all their hot, spicy foods. They gave him hot peppers and hot mustard. They gave him the hottest sausages in the land.

Krakus mixed all the food together. Then
the baker baked it into a pie.

The dragon ate the whole pie.
But the hot, spicy food burned his insides.
He roared, and the mountains shook.
Then he nearly drank the river dry.

The dragon took off, never to be seen again.
The villagers made Krakus their king.
Then they named their village Krakow for
the clever man who had saved one and all.

Responding

Think About the Selection

 What do Krakus and the villagers see when they go down to the river?

2 Give directions to the characters in the story, telling them what they must do each day.

Following Directions

Here are directions Krakus might have given the villagers. Copy them on a piece of paper in the order he would want them done.

Next, help me mix all the spicy food together.

Last, bake this spicy mixture in a pie.

First, bring me all your spicy food.

MY GREEN THUMB

by Maxine Effenson Chuck
illustrated by Mary GrandPré

Strategy Focus

When Isador touches plants, amazing things happen. As you read, **predict** what Isador will do with his strange ability.

My father is a gardener. And now, so am I.
Here's how it happened.

One day I was helping my father in the garden.
Suddenly it started raining. My thumb felt funny.
I looked down and saw that it was green!

When the rain stopped, I helped my father with some tomato plants. In a flash, the tomatoes grew as big as pillows.

"What's going on?" I asked my father.
"I guess those tomatoes *really* needed water,"
my father said. I wasn't so sure.

So I grabbed a sunflower.
It grew as big as an umbrella!
Soon I was high above the garden.

From up there, I picked a rose. It grew as big as a pizza. A bee feasted on the rose. The bee grew as big as a hummingbird!

My mother was amazed.
She said, "Isador, let's not tell anyone about this."
My father said, "Yes, people won't understand."
I said, "But I want to show everyone what I can do."

"Well," said my father, "why don't you grow a pumpkin for the county fair? Then you can show what you can do without telling how you do it!"

It was a great idea. But it wasn't an easy one.
Every pumpkin I grew got much too big to carry.

I needed practice. I started with a carrot. I held the
top. The carrot burst through my fingers. Then it
burst through the kitchen wall.

Next, I tried an onion. It didn't grow as big as the carrot. But its smell was so strong, we cried our eyes out.

Then I grew so many Brussels sprouts,
I had to eat them for a week. Yuck!

At last, I learned how to control my thumb.
I'd give a small green apple a little squeeze, and then
BINGO. A large red apple sat in my hand.

Now I was ready for pumpkins.
I grew them big, but not too big.

I picked out my best pumpkin
and took it to the fair.

The judges said they had never seen such a big
pumpkin. They told me that someday I would be a
great gardener. They didn't know that someday was
already here!

Responding

THINK ABOUT THE SELECTION

1 What happens to Isador's thumb?

2 What makes Isador believe that he is a special gardener?

USE CLUES TO DRAW A CONCLUSION

One way to think about drawing conclusions is to keep a chart like this. Copy the chart on a piece of paper. Then complete the chart by writing more clues that show how having a green thumb can sometimes be a problem.

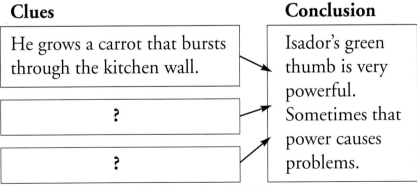

Clues	Conclusion
He grows a carrot that bursts through the kitchen wall.	Isador's green thumb is very powerful. Sometimes that power causes problems.
?	
?	

LUNA

by Philemon Sturges
illustrated by Suling Wang

Strategy Focus

Saul has an unusual pet named Luna.
As you read, **monitor** how well you
follow what happens, and reread to
clarify anything you don't understand.

Luna was a lovely caterpillar. She lived in a glass tank. Every morning, Saul brought Luna leaves to munch.

Saul talked to Luna every day. One day he said, "Luna, my Grandpa's sick. We're going to see him. I wish you could come."

"I wish I could, too," Luna seemed to say.

So Saul asked his mom.

"I'm sorry, Saul. The tank's too big and heavy," she said.

Saul was sad and lonely at Grandpa's house. Grandpa was asleep most of the time. And Saul's mother was busy taking care of Grandpa.

Saul missed Luna. He wanted to tell her how lonely he was.

When they got home, Saul rushed in to see Luna. "Did you miss me?" he asked his caterpillar. Saul looked inside the tank.

Luna was gone. Saul looked all around his room.
No Luna. "Mom!" Saul cried. "Luna is gone!
Why did we have to go to Grandpa's?"

Mom hugged Saul. Then she said, "Grandpa couldn't take care of himself. Luna can. She's probably outside having a great time. But I'm sure she misses you."

That night Saul watched the full moon rise and thought about Luna. Then he thought about Grandpa. And then he fell asleep.

When the moon came to the top of the sky, Saul woke up. A giant moth stood glowing in the moonlight.

"Climb on my back," she said. "Let's go for a ride."

They flew to the moon. Saul looked down. "The earth is magical!" he said.

"So it is," said the moth.

At breakfast Saul told his mother about the giant moth. Mom said, "You were dreaming. Moths don't carry people. And they can't fly to the moon!"

Then she smiled and said, "But sick people *can* get better! Grandpa just called. He took a long walk this morning."

That evening Saul found a rumpled something in the tank. It looked like an old leaf. "I guess that's what's left of Luna," he said to himself.

Suddenly a beautiful moth landed on the table.
It looked just like the moth in his dream, only
much smaller.

"I'm Luna," the moth seemed to say. "I've changed, that's all. But I'll always be your friend."

Then Luna flew into the moonlit night.

Think About the Selection

1. What is Luna at the beginning of the story? What is she at the end?

2. What is Saul's problem at the beginning of the story? What is Saul's problem when he comes home from Grandpa's?

Story Structure

One way to look at the structure of a story is to make a story map. Copy this map on a piece of paper and then complete it.

STORY MAP

Beginning Grandpa is sick, and Saul leaves his caterpillar, Luna, at home.	
Middle	?
End	?